OC 03 '02	DATE DUE		
NO 06 '02	DE 15 '06		
NO 26 '02	DE 20 '06		
MR 27 '03	JA 10 '06		
MY 12 '03	JA 24		
NO 03 '06	MAR 0 1 '10		
DE 17 '04	APR 0 1 '10		
JA 11 '05	APR 19 '10		
OC 24 '05	MAY 2 7 '11		
OC 24 '05			
DE 11 '06			

Infamous Pirates

by

Richard Kozar

Chelsea House Publishers
Philadelphia

CHELSEA HOUSE PUBLISHERS

Editor-in-Chief Stephen Reginald
Managing Editor James D. Gallagher
Production Manager Pamela Loos
Art Director Sara Davis
Picture Editor Judy Hasday
Senior Production Editor Lisa Chippendale
Designers Takeshi Takahashi

First Printing

1 3 5 7 9 8 6 4 2

Library of Congress Cataloging-in-Publication Data

Kozar, Richard.
Infamous pirates / by Richard Kozar.

   p. cm. — (Costume, tradition, & culture: reflecting on the
past)
Includes biographical references and index.
Summary: Profiles twenty-five male and female sea robbers
who stalked oceans from the Spanish Main to the East
Indies, including Henry "John" Avery, Anne Bonny, and Sir
Henry Morgan.

ISBN 0–7910–5165–X (hardcover)
1. Pirates—Biography—Juvenile literature. 2. Buccaneers—Biography—Juvenile literature. [1. Buccaneers.
2. Pirates.] I. Title. II. Series.
G535.K65 1998   [b]98-35722
910.4'5—dc21   CIP
                                  AC

CONTENTS

INTRODUCTION

For as long as people have known that other cultures existed, they have been curious about the differences in their customs and traditions. Julius Caesar, the famous Roman leader, wrote long chronicles about the inhabitants of Gaul (modern-day France) while he was leading troops in the Gallic Wars (58–51 B.C.). In the chronicles, he discussed their religious beliefs, their customs, their day-to-day life, and the conflicts among the different groups. Explorers like Marco Polo traveled thousands of miles and devoted years of their lives to learning about the peoples of the East and bringing home the stories of Chinese court life, along with the silks, spices, and inventions of that culture. The Chelsea House series *Costume, Tradition, and Culture: Reflecting on the Past* continues this legacy of exploration and discovery by discussing some of the most fascinating traditions, beliefs, legends, and artifacts from around the world.

Different cultures develop traditions and costumes to mark the roles of people in their societies, to commemorate events in their histories, and to make the changes and mysteries of life more meaningful. Soldiers wear uniforms to show that they are serving in their nation's army, and insignia on the uniforms show what ranks they hold within the army. People of Bukhara, a city in Uzbekistan, have for centuries woven fine threads of gold into their clothes, and when they travel to other cities they can be recognized as Bukharans by the golden embroidery on their traditional costume. For many years, in the Irish countryside, people would leave bowls of milk outside at night as an offering to the fairies, or "Good People," believing that this would help ensure their favor and keep the family safe from fairy mischief. In Mexico, November 2 is the Day of the Dead, when people visit cemeteries and have feasts to remember their ancestors. In the United States, brides wear white dresses, and the traditional wedding includes many rituals: the father of the bride "giving her away" to the groom, the exchange of vows and rings, the throwing of rice, the tossing of the bride's bouquet. These rituals and symbols help make the marriage meaningful and special for the couple, their families, and their friends, by expressing the change that is taking place and allowing the friends and families to wish luck to the couple.

This series will explore some of the myths, symbols, costumes, and traditions of various cultures from around the world and different times in the past. *Fighting Units of the American War of Independence,* for example, will detail the uniforms, weapons, and decorations of the regiments and battalions on both sides of the war, along with the battles in which they became famous. *Roman Heroes, Myths, and Legends* describes how the ancient Romans explained the wonders and natural phenomena of their world with fantastic stories of superhuman heroes and almost human deities who could change the course of history at will. In *Popular Superstitions,* you will learn how some familiar superstitious beliefs—such as throwing spilled salt over your shoulder, or hanging a horseshoe over your door for good luck—originally began, in times when people feared that devils and evil spirits were meddling in their lives. Few people still believe in malicious spirits, but many still toss the spilled salt over their shoulders, or knock on wood when expressing cautious hope. The legendary figures of a culture—the brave explorers of *The Wild West* or the wicked brigands described in *Infamous Pirates*—help shape that culture's values by providing grand, almost mythical examples of what people should (or should not!) strive to be.

The illustrations that accompany these books have their own cultural history. Originally, they were printed on small collectors' cards and sold in the early 20th century. Each card in a set of 25 or 50 would depict a different person, artifact, or event, and usually the reverse side would offer a few sentences of description to explain the picture. Now, they provide a fascinating glimpse into history and an entertaining addition to the stories presented here.

About the Author

RICHARD KOZAR is a former journalist and newspaper publisher in western Pennsylvania who is now a freelance writer. His latest book for Chelsea House, *Hillary Rodham Clinton,* was published in 1998. He lives with his wife, Heidi, and their daughters, Caty and Macy, near Latrobe, Pennsylvania.

Pirate Infamy

irates have terrified and fascinated the civilized world for centuries. At sea, the appearance of a pirate ship on the horizon meant pirates might board a victim ship and capture, even kill, those aboard. On land, at least in England, you could often see pirates in chains—or swinging from ropes on Execution Dock.

Many of our ideas about piracy come from works of fiction, such as *Peter Pan*. Actually, some pirates *did* look a lot like the villainous Captain Hook—for instance, the dashing Bartholomew Roberts and the terrifying Blackbeard. Some pirates in the 17th, 18th, and even 19th centuries dressed the way we imagine them, but they were also criminals, and a few of them were insane, bloodthirsty rogues who died as violently as they lived.

Fiction has also influenced our idea of the pirate ship. There is only one actual, documented example of a pirate forcing victims to walk the plank. There were far quicker ways to silence people, including cutting them down with a cutlass. And pirates seldom buried their treasure, although Rock the Brazilian, after his capture, admitted he had hidden some booty—which was promptly recovered.

Why would pirates bury their loot? Their only goal was to make money from the spoils they stole, first dividing up the gold, silver, and cargo and then selling it to merchants, often in colonial America.

Only the wisest pirates retired to live a long, comfortable life. Many more wasted their profits in the nearest port. Then off they went to prowl the seas again, a habit that often led to their capture—and ended with a hangman's noose.

CAPT. HENRY "JOHN" AVERY

A member of the Roundsmen—the pirates who mainly sailed in the East Indies at the end of the 17th century—Avery was known as the "Arch Pirate" and "Long Ben." In his day, he was the envy of those who flew under the Jolly Roger.

Among his most famous feats was taking part in the capture of two Arabian ships in the Red Sea. Richly stocked with gold, silver, and important Muslim pilgrims returning from Mecca, the *Fateh Mohamed* and the *Ganj-I-Sawai* were loaded with riches beyond Avery's wildest dreams. The *Ganj-I-Sawai* was also loaded with cannon and riflemen. But fate was on Avery's side: the pirates boarded the ship after a pirate cannon ball brought down its mainmast, which created panic on the deck. Within two hours, the ship was Avery's.

The two ships carried 500,000 gold and silver coins, chest after chest crammed with jewels, and a jewel-encrusted saddle intended for the great Mogul, a descendant of the

conquering ruler of India. When such important ships were seized by pirates, governments from India to London went into action. The English government offered a reward of 500 pounds—an amount the average merchant seaman might make in an entire life at sea.

Avery sailed back to the Caribbean Sea. Here he hoped the English governors, who had proven to be fairly lenient toward pirates, would allow him to live safely. He found little protection, because his greatest conquest had also made him too well-known and feared for his own good.

Long Ben did manage to avoid authorities—and the hangman's noose. Several of his crew did not. The tale that got around was that Long Ben retired to Ireland.

CAPT. SAMUEL BELLAMY

apt. "Black Sam" Bellamy became a threat to trade ships from the Caribbean to coastal Canada beginning about 1716. This was because in 1715, a hurricane sank 12 Spanish galleons off the coast of Florida, along with 14 million pesos of treasure. The watery treasure drew treasure hunters to the region the way blood in the sea draws sharks.

The hundreds of seamen who joined in the pillaging became known as the "Flying Gang." They used an island in the Bahamas, New Providence, as their base. The tropical island, described as a "Nest of Pyrates," was a buccaneer's dream: it sheltered hundreds of pirate vessels but was too shallow for warships.

Bellamy was an Englishman who had abandoned his family for a pirate's life. He is credited with capturing 50 vessels. "I am a free prince and I have as much authority to make war on the whole World as he who has a hundred sail

of ships at sea and 100,000 men in the field," he lectured the captain of one plundered ship. Bellamy was also known as "the Orator" because he loved making speeches.

What was the worst disaster Bellamy ever caused? The wreck of his own 28-gun flagship, the *Whydah Galley*. During a violent storm, he drove it onto a shoal off Cape Cod, Massachusetts, as his crew drank Madeira wine. In the wreckage, discovered by modern treasure hunters in 1984, were the ship's bell and a treasure trove of gold and silver.

Maj. Stede Bonnet

he life of a pirate attracted all types. Major Stede Bonnet left the comfortable life of a retired English military officer and Barbados sugar plantation overseer for thrills as a pirate on the high seas. His decision to change careers shocked his upper-class family and friends. It probably surprised quite a few pirates as well.

In the first place, Bonnet did not look like a pirate. Instead of an intimidating captain brandishing pistols in each hand and wearing an eyepatch, he was a portly gentleman with a powdered wig, a satin coat, and spotless breeches. In the early 18th century, he was what people called a "dandy."

And even more out of character for a pirate, and in a notable lapse of pirate etiquette, Bonnet *paid for* his 10-gun sloop, the *Revenge,* and outfitted it with an inexperienced crew. Any pirate knew the way to get a ship was to capture

one outright, and the way to get a good crew was to commandeer seasoned sailors. Perhaps the most remarkable of Bonnet's acts was going into partnership with Edward Teach, the dreaded "Blackbeard."

Blackbeard instantly recognized Bonnet as a sheep in sheep's clothing, even though Bonnet had captured a few ships on his own. Teach's low opinion of Bonnet was evident to everyone but the major himself, when Teach put his own lieutenant in charge of his so-called partner's ship, relieving Bonnet of his own vessel and command.

Eventually, Teach tired of Bonnet's inept pirating. He stripped Bonnet's ship and stranded his 25-man crew. Bonnet was later captured and tried in a Charleston, South Carolina, court. Despite his pathetic pleas for mercy, he and 28 other pirates were hanged in 1718.

ANNE BONNY

Famous even as a child for her fiery temper, Anne Bonny was the daughter of a respected lawyer from County Cork, Ireland, who emigrated to Charlestown, South Carolina. When she was 13, her rage boiled over and she stabbed a servant girl with a knife. Anne ran away from her new home, leaving behind a hefty inheritance, to marry James Bonny, a sailor with few prospects. The couple moved to New Providence, an island in the Bahamas where many pirates hid out.

On New Providence, Anne deserted her husband and married a pirate, Capt. John Rackham. She donned men's clothes and went aboard Rackham's ship as his "cabin boy" to keep their relationship secret.

The pirate couple seized a Dutch ship and crew. Bonny especially liked one of the young crew members, a "boy" who turned out to be an Englishwoman, Mary Read. Driven by her own lust for adventure, Mary had been a cabin boy

on a military warship, an infantryman, and a calvaryman, each time disguised as a man. After Mary's husband died, she had joined the Dutch ship as a merchantman.

When Bonny told her husband, Captain Rackham, that Mary Read was in fact a young woman, he permitted Read to join the pirates, which she apparently did with gusto. From documented accounts, Anne and Mary fought "like wildcats" during battles, especially when their ship was finally captured in 1720.

Tried separately from the men of the crew, Anne and Mary both escaped hanging, because they were both pregnant. What finally happened to Anne Bonny after the trial remains unknown.

CAPT. CHRISTOPHER CONDENT

hristopher Condent hailed originally from Plymouth, Massachusetts, like many other pirates who sailed the Pirate Round. The Round was a trade route used to transport goods from the east coast of Africa, particularly Madagascar, to ports in the Caribbean and the colonies on America's east coast.

By the early 1700s, the pirate trade along the Caribbean and North American trade routes was dying down, because of severe crackdowns on pirates and their strongholds. But ships carrying far greater treasures along India's Malabar Coast and the adjacent Red Sea became tempting targets for pirates like Condent. He was one of the first to flee North American waters when the pirate stronghold on New Providence was wiped out in 1718.

On his way to the East Indies, Condent looted several ships. The richest was perhaps an Arab vessel off Bombay

carrying a fortune in gold and silver. Condent and his crew retreated to safe harbor at Madagascar and split up their booty, worth thousands of English pounds. So bounteous was the haul that they left a sizable portion lying on the beach.

Wisely, Condent and 40 of his men decided to forsake the risky business of piracy and retire. Some of his crew settled on an island off Madagascar, where the French governor granted them pardons for their crimes at sea. Condent fared particularly well for a career pirate: he married the governor's sister-in-law and became a prosperous shipowner on the coast of France.

CAPT. HOWELL DAVIS

Before he turned to a life of crime at sea, Howell Davis served as mate on a slave ship. When the ship was captured by Edward England, an Irish pirate sailing across the Atlantic from Nassau to Madagascar, Davis became a pirate himself, another member of the Roundsmen—the pirates who pillaged the East Indies.

Although his plundering began in the West Indies, Davis—like Captain Condent— soon set his sights on the treasure-laden East Indies, especially the African coast. He earned a reputation for bold strategy, often taking his victims by surprise and intimidating them by his superior numbers—even when the victims actually outnumbered his men.

This fearlessness ultimately led to Davis's undoing. He had a string of successful strikes at merchant ships off the coast of Africa, including the looting of a richly laden Dutch

vessel. Davis decided to attack next not a ship but a Portuguese settlement on Prince's Island in the Guinea Gulf—a settlement guarded by a fort. He drew up a careful plan to overwhelm the forces manning the fort, but news of his plot reached the island. After Davis and several companions received a cordial welcome from the Portuguese governor, they were gunned down in an ambush.

Davis may be best known for inspiring Bartholomew Roberts, or "Black Bart," to become a legendary pirate himself. Roberts was serving as second mate aboard the English ship *Princess,* headed from London to the Guinea Coast for a load of slaves, when it was attacked and seized by Davis off the coast of West Africa. After Davis's death, Roberts became captain and destroyed the Portuguese settlement on Prince's Island in revenge.

CAPT. EDWARD ENGLAND

ot all pirates were murderous villains who died as violently as they lived. Edward "Ned" England, for example, hardly fits the mold. An Irishman who practiced the pirate's trade in the Caribbean before New Providence was cleansed of pirates in 1718, he is described as "having a great deal of good nature . . . courageous, not over-avaricious, humane, but too often overruled." Overruled by whom? His "wicked associates," says one record.

England gave up plying his trade in the New World and set sail for the East Indies, where he formed an alliance with Capt. John Taylor, who was as ruthless as England was good-natured. After seizing several ships in the Indian Ocean, the pair retreated to an island visited by trade ships as well as by pirates.

In the harbor there, Taylor and England discovered two English merchant ships. One managed to escape, stranding

the other, the *Cassandra,* commanded by James Macrae. Although the English fought bravely, over a dozen of Macrae's crew were killed in the battle, and twice as many were wounded, including Macrae himself. Taylor would have finished Macrae off, but the nobler England intervened. He spared the severely wounded officer, who was allowed to sail a badly damaged ship to India, where he recovered.

England's good deed turned his crew against him. They thought he was too meek, and they mutinied. Set adrift in a small launch, England miraculously made his way to Madagascar, where he died shortly thereafter.

CAPT. WIILLIAM FLY

apt. William Fly was a brutal pirate, never content unless plotting some attack or misdeed. In 1726, for example, as a boatswain sailing from Jamaica on the sloop *Elizabeth,* Fly instigated a mutiny in which the crew murdered Capt. John Green and mate Thomas Jenkins by throwing them overboard. Then the crew began terrorizing merchant ships.

While cruising the New England coast, Fly and his crew were overcome by prisoners they were holding aboard the ship. The former prisoners promptly delivered them all in chains to Boston, which was the last city many pirates ever visited. In 1724, for instance, the *Boston Gazette* had reported: "On Tuesday the 2nd instant, were executed here for piracy John Rose Archer, Quarter-Master, aged about 27 years, and William White, aged about 22 years: After their Death, they were conveyed in boats down to an island where

White was buried, and the Quarter-Master was hung up in irons, to be a spectacle, and so a warning to others."

But Fly defied his captors to the end. After he was convicted of piracy, Fly and his crew were counseled on the evil of their ways by the Reverend Cotton Mather, a famous American clergyman. Fly was not impressed, and he refused to attend the meeting house worship led by Mather the Sunday before Fly's scheduled execution.

Fly showed up at his own hanging carrying a small bouquet of flowers. As he climbed the stairs of the gallows, he traded remarks with bystanders. He is even supposed to have instructed the hangman on the proper way to set the noose on one's neck. If Mather and the other law-abiding citizens of Boston expected Fly to repent, like many of his fellow pirates he sorely disappointed his reformers.

PIERRE
FRANÇOIS

French buccaneer, or pirate, Pierre François
was active around the 1630s, operating from
the stronghold of Tortuga, a small island
between Hispaniola and Cuba. Like the island
of New Providence a half century later, Tortuga was a pirate
refuge. There buccaneers found fresh water, harbors easy to
defend, and a strategic launching point near an important
trade route. The Spanish occasionally tried to wipe out the
pirates who sought shelter on the island, but with little success.

Showing unusual wisdom for pirates, Pierre le Grand
and several other French pirates of Tortuga seized ships filled
with impressive treasure, then left Spanish merchant vessels
alone. In François's case, however, greed won out over better
judgment. With a crew of 26 men, he sailed south in an
open boat toward Venezuela to raid pearling boats off the
coast of South America. François found the pearling fleet—a

dozen canoes occupied by black divers—protected by two Spanish warships

Incredibly, François's crew managed to sail right up to the smaller warship by pretending to be a friendly group of local seamen. When they approached within striking distance, a fight broke out, which François's crew won. They found 100,000 pieces of silver aboard the Spanish ship, a prize rich enough for almost any pirate.

Thirsting for even more treasure, however, François and his men attacked the second warship, a move that turned out to be as foolhardy as it was bold. Even so, the clever Frenchman came to surrender terms with the Spaniards, thereby saving the lives of himself and his crew.

CAPT. JOHN GOW

M utiny was a convenient tactic for disgruntled or power-hungry seamen lured by the freedom and profits of piracy. Scotsman John Gow was 35 when he became a mutineer. The year was 1724, and a ship named the *George Galley* was embarking from the Canary Islands for the Strait of Gibraltar.

The second mate and gunner, Gow had signed on with the *George Galley* specifically to hatch his plot at sea. Before midnight on November 3, he and his villainous team attacked the ship's doctor, chief mate, and clerk, slashing their throats as the men slept.

Then the mutineers turned their sights above deck, where they found Capt. Oliver Ferneau, who put up a vicious fight even after they had cut his throat. Ferneau didn't go down for good until one of the mutineers shot him at point-blank range. The mutineers dumped all four bodies overboard.

Though not every man aboard the *George Galley* was in cahoots with Gow's gang, the average seaman in those days usually had little choice but to join his new pirate leaders after such a mutiny—at least until he was close enough to a port to make his escape.

After seizing several merchant ships, Gow steered his newly named ship, the *Revenge,* to Scotland, where one of his own crew members led to his undoing by notifying local authorities. Gow was captured and shipped to England, where he and eight crewmen were found guilty of murder and piracy and hanged.

CAPT.
JOHN HALSEY

ike many buccaneers during the golden age of piracy, Capt. John Halsey was active in the first decade of the 1700s. Born in Boston, he spent most of his career as a pirate in the East Indies, particularly the Indian Ocean and Red Sea. He made a point of not attacking European vessels, a practice that both harmed and saved him.

Halsey commanded the 10-gun ship *Charles* beginning in 1705, heading for Madagascar. By the next year, he was ousted as captain for refusing to attack a larger vessel the *Charles* had been stalking. Although his crew presumed their target was a merchant ship like any other, Halsey recognized it as Dutch and recommended calling off the attack. His stubborn crew argued—until the Dutch ship turned and fired its cannon. All talk of their captain's cowardice ended, and Halsey assumed the helm once again.

Halsey's chastened crew hesitated to attack larger vessels

from that point on, but in 1707 Halsey engaged a British squadron of five ships carrying 62 guns. His bold advance sent the largest ship sailing for safety, leaving the others to fend for themselves. Halsey captured two of them and seized 50,000 pounds of cash and goods.

Like many pirates, Halsey didn't enjoy his triumph for long. A year later, a hurricane caught the *Charles* and the ships Halsey had captured and destroyed them all. Captain Halsey came down with a fever not long afterward, died in Madagascar, and was honored with a hero's burial.

CAPT. WILLIAM KIDD

aptain Kidd is the most famous swashbuckler in pirate lore. In truth he was a mediocre pirate, although a unique one.

Born in Scotland in 1655, the son of a Presbyterian minister, Kidd was commanding the English ship *Blessed William* in the West Indies in 1691 when his crew mutinied. They left him stranded on the island of Antigua, but he somehow managed to sail to New York City. There, his fortunes reversed after he married a wealthy widow who lived on Wall Street.

Restless for the sea, Kidd petitioned King William III and received command of a 34-gun privateering ship. He felt this gave him the legal right to seize French ships and their cargo. He was also expected to raid pirate vessels, which were draining the king's profits. His only real chance to profit from the venture, though, was to turn pirate himself, which he ultimately did by capturing the *Quedah Mer-*

chant, an Indian vessel loaded with hundreds of thousands of pounds in riches.

Back in England, government authorities denounced Kidd as a pirate rather than a hired privateer, and they put a price on his head from New England to the West Indies. Fearing for his life, Kidd made his way back to Boston in 1699, selling and hiding treasure along the way from the Caribbean to New York. Despite his protests of innocence to his chief backer in Boston, Kidd was clapped in irons and eventually sent to England for trial.

In England, Captain Kidd was found guilty of piracy and murder and hanged on May 23, 1701.

MICHAEL LE BASQUE

ichael le Basque, a Frenchman, was already enjoying the rewards of a successful marauder's life on the island of Tortuga when he formed an alliance with one of the most villainous barbarians to run up a black flag. His partner was Jean-David Nau, more commonly known as François L'Olonnois.

A sadistic pirate with no pity for his victims or even for his shipmates, L'Olonnois had a reputation for finding out quickly whether treasure was hidden aboard a captured ship: Should his unfortunate prisoners be slow to reveal the whereabouts of treasure, he would slash them with his cutlass, burn them with matches, or even squeeze their heads with rope until their eyes bulged out, a practice called *woolding*. Sickened by L'Olonnois's cruel tactics, some of his own men jumped ship.

Together, le Basque and L'Olonnois assembled a fleet equipped with several hundred of Tortuga's seasoned rovers.

They sailed the Spanish Main—the Caribbean Sea, along the American mainland—for the Venezuelan port of Maracaibo, pillaging Spanish ships along the way. The band of buccaneers turned Maracaibo and its terrified inhabitants inside out for days in search of treasure. Then they attacked another prosperous port town, Gibraltar, which surrendered after hundreds of Spanish troops died. L'Olonnois and le Basque sacked Gibraltar for more than a month.

After his reign along the Spanish Main, no record exists of le Basque. But L'Olonnois's demise is well documented. He was captured by the Indians he had besieged time and again; they burned him and scattered his ashes.

CAPT.
EDWARD LOW

nglish-born Edward Low was one of the cruelest pirates ever to run under the Jolly Roger—his own banner was a blood-red skeleton on a black background. As just one example: When the captain of a captured Portuguese merchant ship threw a bag of gold coins overboard, Low cut off the man's lips and broiled them in front of him. Low then murdered the ship's entire crew.

A hardened criminal by the time he was a teen, Low worked in a New England shipyard before his bizarre behavior cost him his job. Like many who had neither the education nor the character to live among more civilized citizens, Low found his way to the Caribbean—and a rewarding life as a pirate.

The mere mention of his name bred terror across the trade routes. Low was even more intimidating in person—he

had a livid scar across his face made by the inadvertent slash of a drunken crewman attempting to strike a prisoner.

Cold-hearted as he was, Low was a husband and father, although he allowed none of his crew to have families. Interrogating prisoners to learn if they were married, he once threatened to shoot a man if he didn't answer. When the prisoners confessed that none had spouses, Low relaxed. He had deserted his wife and young child in Boston, leading one prisoner to suspect the pirate would not allow married men on board because they might someday desert the ship to return to their family.

No one knows for certain how the cruel captain met his fate.

Capt. George Lowther

eorge Lowther was a partner in crime with Capt. Edward Low, who was as ruthless a buccaneer as ever sailed. Lowther was scarcely better. He led a mutiny as a second mate aboard an English merchant ship transporting slaves in 1721. Because seamen hated the heat, disease, and boredom a trip to Africa entailed, they were easy to persuade. Lowther provided the spark, convincing the crew to seize control of the *Gambia Castle,* elect him captain, and sail for the Caribbean.

More than 100 members of the ship's crew who refused to take part in the mutiny were left behind in Africa. Within a year, nearly three-quarters of them died of fever.

Lowther ran into Low in the Cayman Islands, which had a reputation as a pirate refuge, and subsequently made Low a lieutenant. Both were uncommonly cruel: Lowther made tight-lipped captives reveal their secrets by setting burning gunner's matches between their fingers.

But even scoundrels like Lowther could not count on being lucky forever. After his lieutenant broke away to begin his own buccaneering enterprise, Lowther's ship was nearly destroyed—an English merchant ship off South Carolina battled harder than the pirates expected. Repairs took nearly an entire winter.

When Lowther next turned up in the West Indies, his luck went even more sour. While his ship lay careened ashore (on its side for scraping and repair of the wooden hull), he was surprised by a party of merchantmen sailing the *Eagle*. Most of his crew were killed or captured. Lowther apparently killed himself with his own pistol.

Sir Henry Morgan

Welsh pirate Henry Morgan, born in 1635, became one of the most skillful and successful seagoing marauders on the Spanish Main.

Morgan organized hundreds of buccaneers in 1668 in a fleet of over a dozen ships and ransacked what is now Camaguey, Cuba. He convinced the populace to reveal their hidden valuables by a favorite method of pirate persuasion—torture. Months later his followers stormed Puerto Bello, one of the richest but most fortified prizes in the region. Faced with superior force, Morgan preached a mixture of courage and greed: "If our number is small, our hearts are great; and the fewer persons we are, the more union, and the better shares we shall have in the spoil!"

The fearless buccaneer systematically overran the heavily armed fortresses of Puerto Bello, including the governor's stockade. He then tortured the residents until they turned over a mountain of silver, gold, and jewels. The loot included

500,000 pieces of eight (Spanish silver coins each worth one real, or an eighth of a peso).

But Morgan mounted his boldest attack in 1670 when he rounded up a fleet of 40 ships manned by 2,000 buccaneers. His target? Panama City, one of the richest ports in the New World. To reach the Pacific port, Morgan and most of his force had to canoe and walk over the Isthmus of Panama. Unfortunately for him, the first thing he saw as he approached the city was a Spanish galleon loaded with gold, leaving the harbor. Worse, the military defenders burned most of the town rather than leave it to Morgan.

Despite attempts by official England to reign Morgan in, an adoring public convinced Charles II to knight the buccaneer instead.

BARTHOLEMY PORTUGUEZ

lthough most pirates were English, Bartholemy Portuguez (sometimes called the Portuguese Bartholemy) hailed from Portugal, which also warred with Spain. Rather than be known as a *buccaneer*, he and other Portuguese pirates preferred the label *flibustier*, a French version of the word *freebooter*.

Portuguez came to the Caribbean with a modest crew in a small ship armed with four cannons. Who knows why he felt compelled to attack a Spanish man-of-war in his first big confrontation? But he did attack, after the Spanish commander emptied 10 of his cannon at the small craft without a single hit. Portuguez's men scrambled aboard the warship and fought hand to hand but were repulsed and had to retreat. They then proceeded to harass the Spaniards with rifle fire, picking off crewmen one by one as they tried to sail the ship.

Again Portuguez's men boarded, and this time the flibustiers won the day, although they lost many crewmen in the process. Nonetheless, the prize they captured was rich; the man-of-war's hull was loaded with 75,000 pieces of gold.

Before Portuguez's crew could celebrate, they sailed straight into a Spanish fleet, whose crews boarded them, reclaimed their prize, and imprisoned the hapless flibustiers. Bartholemy was to be hung in a nearby port.

In one of the greatest escapes in pirate history, Bartholemy killed his jailer on ship the night before he was scheduled to be hung, jumped overboard, and swam to shore, holding onto sealed wine jars to stay afloat. Moreover, to reach safety, he then slogged through more than a hundred miles of treacherous swamp.

CAPT. JOHN "JACK" RACKHAM

ore commonly known as "Calico Jack" for the striped pants he wore, John Rackham began his pirate ways as quartermaster for Capt. Charles Vane. A quartermaster, who ranked nearly as high as the captain on pirate ships, was expected to lead the attacks when storming merchant vessels. But after Rackham accused Vane of cowardice for not attacking a French ship, Rackham himself was elected captain.

Calico Jack was by most pirate measures a small and benign operator. He once returned a looted Maderian ship to its master. In fact, Rackham's main claim to fame comes not from his own exploits, but from those of two pirates who sailed with him—his wife, Anne Bonny, and her friend Mary Read.

After receiving a royal pardon in 1719 on New Providence, Calico Jack courted Bonny and convinced her to leave her unimposing husband. Then, yearning to return to

piracy, he married Bonny, had a child, and took his wife—dressed as a man—to sea with him. They were soon joined by Mary Read, another woman dressed as a man, whom Rackham captured along with the rest of a crew of a merchant ship.

After stealing the sloop *William* from Nassau harbor, Rackham and his female partners incurred the wrath of Woodes Rogers, the Bahamas governor who had granted Calico Jack's pardon. Now Rogers declared Rackham and his band pirates, and they were hunted down.

Rackham hanged with the male members of his crew. The two women, who were both pregnant, were spared.

MARY READ

ary Read is notorious for being one of two female pirates in the West Indies. She spent much of her life at sea disguised as a man. Small wonder—she was raised as a boy.

Read's mother was an Englishwoman whose husband ran off to sea, leaving her with a son. She became pregnant with Mary from an illicit affair, after her husband deserted her. She moved out of town to give birth to her out-of-wedlock daughter in secret. Then her son died, and Mary's mother found herself not only depressed but nearly penniless. In order to save her daughter, Mary, her mother dressed her as a boy, then convinced her mother-in-law—her absent husband's mother—to support her new "grandson."

At age 13, when other young girls of her class might have become chambermaids, Mary became a footman. But she soon tired of the dull job and joined the army, disguised of course as a man. After a brief marriage to a fellow soldier,

during which she lived as a woman, she again donned men's clothing and sailed on a ship headed for the West Indies. The ship was seized by the pirate Calico Jack Rackham and his wife, Anne Bonny, coincidentally another woman dressed for concealment in men's clothes.

Bonny at first took Mary Read for a handsome lad. When she discovered the truth, she encouraged Read to join herself and her husband as a pirate. The trio's partnership at sea was short-lived. They were captured and sentenced to death. Because Bonny and Mary Read were pregnant, both escaped hanging. Read died soon afterward in prison.

CAPT. BARTHOLOMEW ROBERTS

oberts was arguably the best pirate of his day. Always handsomely dressed, the Welshman combined a flair for adventure with fine seamanship. Known as the "Great Pyrate Roberts" or simply "Black Bart," he inspired admiration among his followers and terror among his prey.

Unlike pirates such as Captain Kidd, who didn't deserve their reputations as great pirates, Roberts actually carried out the exploits he became famous for. In 1720, sailing in a single sloop off the Newfoundland coast, his small band surprised 22 ships carrying over 1,000 men. Roberts burned all but one ship, on which he stored his booty, then sailed from the harbor only to meet a sizable French fleet, which he promptly sank.

Roberts became a pirate after serving as second mate aboard the *Princess,* an English ship captured by Capt. Howell Davis off the coast of West Africa. Roberts lost his new

captain less than two months later when Davis was killed in a trap set by the governor of Prince's Island in the Guinea Gulf.

Because of his mariner's skill, Roberts was elected captain after Davis's death, which he immediately revenged by annihilating the Portuguese settlement on Prince's Island. He then sailed across the Atlantic to South America, where he plundered the Portuguese vice-admiral's 40-gun ship before any of the 41 vessels surrounding it could retaliate. His haul included 40,000 gold coins and a gold cross inlaid with diamonds, meant for the king of Portugal.

Roberts even managed to die a dramatic death at sea. He was killed by a cannon blast fired by the HMS *Swallow*, an English ship sent to destroy him.

ROCK THE
BRAZILIAN

Rock the Brazilian, whose true name was Roche Brasiliano and whose nationality was actually Dutch, ranks among the most ruthless of pirates. He earned his nickname after moving to the Dutch colony of Bahia in Brazil, then on to Jamaica, where English buccaneers called him Rock. He is the only pirate whom documents report to have actually ever buried treasure.

Rock's short temper was legendary, as were his homicidal tendencies. When drunk, he would run through the streets of towns beating hapless passersby or slashing them with his cutlass. He is also credited with burning alive Spanish prisoners who refused to divulge information to him. Legend has it that mothers in the Caribbean frightened their children into going to sleep by warning them that Rock would get them if they didn't.

In typical pirate fashion, Brasiliano had no sooner pil-

laged a ship and made off with its treasures than he and his crew would sail into some nearby port and drink or squander their new fortune. Indeed, this unquenchable lust for easy money nearly got Rock summarily executed by the Spanish, who captured him on a scouting mission in Campeche.

Rock's cunning, rather than his fearlessness, saved the day. He convinced the Spanish governor to release his crew by delivering a letter the pirate had forged in the name of a fictitious ally—a French captain anchored in the harbor.

The governor released Rock and his crew and sent them to Spain. Rock promptly returned to a life of piracy in the West Indies.

EDWARD TEACH (BLACKBEARD)

Perhaps no other buccaneer played pirate to the hilt like Edward Teach, alias "Blackbeard." His very countenance sent shivers along the spines of early settlers, with "that large quantity of hair, which, like a frightful meteor, covered his whole face, and frightened America more than any comet that has appeared there in a long time," wrote Charles Johnson in his *General History of Pyrates*.

To make himself even more ferocious during battle, Teach used special effects—long, lighted gunner's matches sticking out from under his hat—and wore three brace of pistols hung from bandoleers.

Thought to have come to the Caribbean as a deckhand on a privateering ship, Blackbeard earned his crossbones under Capt. Benjamin Hornigold, who sailed the Dutch vessel *Ranger*. In 1717, after the pair seized a rich French ship sailing from Africa with gold, jewels, and slaves, Blackbeard

was given the prize Dutch ship, which he renamed *Queen Anne's Revenge.*

The "Spawn of the Devil" terrorized shipping lanes throughout the Caribbean and coastal America, eventually drawing the wrath of Governor Spotswood of Virginia, who personally financed a ship and crew to end Blackbeard's devilry. The HMS *Pearl,* commanded by Robert Maynard, cornered Teach in Ocracoke Inlet, North Carolina, and the crews fought fiercely. Blackbeard fired and missed Maynard at close range, but Maynard's answering shot hit home.

Staggering from gun and stab wounds, Teach still nearly ran his cutlass through Maynard, whose own sword had broken. But a navy man slashed the pirate's throat at the last second, and the wild-eyed Blackbeard watched his own lifeblood flow away. As a warning to other pirates, Blackbeard's severed head was placed on the bowsprit of his ship.

CAPT.
THOMAS TEW

ike many pirates, Thomas Tew began his career as a privateer, a mariner licensed by his country to board and seize the cargo of enemy ships in times of war. England commissioned many privateers to harass the ships of its least-favorite nation, Spain. However, like droves of his fellow buccaneers, Tew quickly crossed the thin line that separated privateer from pirate.

In 1692, Tew was sailing aboard the *Amity*, a ship commissioned by Bermuda merchants to seize a French trading post in West Africa. The *Amity* was barely out of port when Tew questioned the wisdom of the voyage—and the possibility of dying to profit other men. He convinced his shipmates to profit themselves instead. They are said to have replied: "A gold chain or a wooden leg, we'll stand by you."

The *Amity* headed around the southern tip of Africa for the Red Sea, where, after several months, the crew stumbled

across the flagship of the Great Mogul of India, loaded with 100,000 pounds of gold, silver, gemstones, and ivory. It was a huge prize, which Tew and his men divided on the island of Madagascar.

When the *Amity* sailed back into Rhode Island, a traditionally hospitable New England port for pirates, the crew received a hero's welcome. Of course, the town's profit-hungry merchants welcomed the chance to buy up the loot as well.

Despite this enormous early success, Tew's tenure as a pirate was a short one. While attacking another Mogul fleet with Capt. Henry Avery, Tew was killed by a cannonball through the belly.

Capt. Charles Vane

here came a time in 1718 when King George I of England grew so alarmed over piracy in the Caribbean that he commissioned Woodes Rogers, a worldly mariner and former privateer, as governor of the Bahamas. Rogers's main job was to bribe buccaneers with the promise of pardons if they swore off sea robbing for good. Their alternative? Capture and death by hanging.

Charles Vane headed a band among the thousand or so pirates enjoying the safety of Nassau, a settlement in the Bahamas, who not only resented Rogers but were determined to neither mend their ways nor end up lynched.

Vane's gang set fire to a captured French ship laden with explosives, then let it drift unmanned toward Rogers's fleet of English ships. The resulting explosions sent lead balls of all shapes and sizes hurtling into the air and lit up the sky, creat-

ing enough of a diversion for Vane and his crew to slip away unnoticed.

They escaped with heaps of loot and avoided capture. But in 1719, Vane cruised south of Jamaica straight into the teeth of a killer hurricane. The wind drove his ship into an uninhabited island, where the vessel broke apart, tossing many of his men into the stormy seas to die.

Vane, who managed to survive, was picked up by an ex-buccaneer, a bit of luck that saved his life only temporarily. He was handed over to naval authorities in Jamaica and hanged at Gallows Point, the same site where Capt. Calico Jack Rackham swung.

VANHORN

In the early days of buccaneering, Vanhorn was among a group of international sea robbers who teamed up to attack Veracruz, a coastal port in what is now Mexico. The year was 1683, and Vanhorn and four other Dutch captains had joined forces with the Chevalier de Grammont, a French nobleman. De Grammont had already seized one particularly prosperous vessel and squandered the proceeds on wine, women, and gambling on the island of Hispaniola. This group of pirates belonged to a loose confederation known as the Brethren of the Coast, and their island refuge was Tortuga.

Vanhorn had sailed to the Caribbean aboard a slave ship hauling human cargo from the Guinea Coast of West Africa. One of his partners was a fellow Dutchman named Laurens de Graaf, who was feared by Spaniards throughout the

region for his ruthless attacks on colonial outposts. He was a veteran seaman with several sizable captures to his credit.

Together, the band of international rogues and nearly 800 crewmen crammed into two ships disguised as Spanish vessels. The ships sailed peacefully into Veracruz, whose residents were awaiting the arrival of two genuine Spanish merchant ships.

Once safely inside the harbor's defenses, the huge pirate force easily overwhelmed the city, capturing enough silver to earn themselves 800 pieces of silver each. But when Vanhorn demanded 30 shares—24,000 pieces—for supplying the two pirate ships, he and de Graaf got into a scrap. Although Vanhorn was only wounded slightly on the wrist, he later developed a blood infection that killed him.

CHRONOLOGY

3000 B.C.	First recorded act of piracy.
330 B.C.	Alexander the Great wages war against piracy.
264 B.C.	Romans and Carthaginians battle over pirates.
78 B.C.	Julius Caesar kidnapped by pirates.
67 B.C.	Roman general Pompey launches 10-year campaign to wipe out Mediterranean pirates.
455 A.D.	Vandal pirates sack Rome.
1573	German pirate Klein Henszlein caught and beheaded.
1630	Buccaneers turn Tortuga into pirate sanctuary.
1640	Pierre le Grand commits first act of buccaneering against the Spanish.
1678	*Buccaneers of America* published by Alexander Esquemelin.
1698	Capt. William Kidd captures *Quedah Merchant*.
1700	Kidd arrested in Boston; hanged a year later in London.
1718	Blackbeard cornered and killed in Ocracoke Inlet. Woodes Rogers levels pirate stronghold at New Providence.
1722	Bartholomew Roberts killed by cannon in battle; 52 pirates of his crew convicted in Admiralty Trials and hanged in West Africa.

1724   Daniel Defoe writes *A General History of the Pyrates,* and Charles Johnson publishes *A General History of the Robberies and Murders of the Most Notorious Pyrates.*

1883   Robert Louis Stevenson writes *Treasure Island.*

1904   J. M. Barrie's play *Peter Pan* is first performed.

1984   Remnants and treasure of Capt. Samuel Bellamy's *Whydah Galley* discovered off Cape Cod.

INDEX ✤

FURTHER READING

Cordingly, David. *Pirates: Terror on the High Seas, from the Caribbean to the South China Sea*. Atlanta: Turner, 1996.

—————. *Under the Black Flag*. New York: Random House, 1995.

Feder, Joshua B. *Pirates*. New York: Michael Friedman, 1992

Lincoln, Margarette. *The Pirate's Handbook*. New York: Cobblehill Books, 1995.

Stockton, Frank R. *Buccaneers and Pirates of Our Coasts*. New York: Macmillan, 1967.